Joanne & Bob
Christmas 1991

Grace & Bob

AMAZING GRACE

AMAZING GRACE

Hymn by John Newton
Introduction by Judy Collins

NEW YORK

Library of Congress Cataloging-in-Publication Data

Amazing grace : [photographs] hymn by John Newton / introduction by Judy Collins. — 1st ed.
p. cm.
ISBN 1-56282-998-X : $15.95 ($19.95 Can.)
1. Amazing grace (Hymn) I. Newton, John, 1725–1807.
BV317.A49A53 1991
264'.2—dc20 91-22927
CIP

Produced by Rapid Transcript, a division of March Tenth, Inc.

FIRST EDITION

10 9 8 7 6 5 4 3 2 1

All photographs are Courtesy of the Daniel J. Ransohoff Collection of the Cincinnati Historical Society except the following:

Page 17: © FPG International. Page 19: © J. K.-Magnum. Page 27: © FPG International. Page 33: © Costa Manos. Page 35: © 1989 Mike Valeri. Page 37: © Billy E. Barnes. Page 51: © Erich Hartmann. Page 53: © Chris Steele. Page 55: © 1975 John Lewis Stage. Page 57: © Magnum.

To Grace, she'll know.

ACKNOWLEDGMENTS

Ken Johnson for his keen eyes and patience.

Ann Kerman for filling in the blanks.

Laura Chace and Linda Bailey of the Cincinnati Historical Society for unlocking the vaults.

Dennis Luzuriaga for his knowing and steady hands.

Father Hank Myers of Vanderbilt University for his trust.

Grace Zobeck for her perfect darkroom.

AMAZING GRACE

A Personal History

Amazing Grace is a song about letting go, bottoming out, seeing the light, turning it over, trusting the universe, breathing in, breathing out, going with the flow; timing is everything, trust your instincts, don't push the river, ease on down the road, get on your knees, let your guard down, drop your defenses, lighten up, like angels they know how to fly, don't be afraid, when all else fails, pray; there are a million ways to say it. If we don't, we crack up, break our hearts.

My friend Rachel Taylor, an actress from the West, tells a story that has always sent chills through me: about the ranching woman who was driving a team of horses, sitting up there on the seat of the pretty buggy flatboard, holding the reins just so behind the prancers. Something spooked the pair and they took off. She held on. Onlookers on the porch of the ranch house cried to her, "Let go! Let go of the reins," but she couldn't let go. The team broke away from the buggy with her still holding on to the reins, and dragged her to her death, pulling out her arms. The antidote for that story, in my mind, is something else I have heard Rachel say: "When you get to the end of your rope, let go."

Amazing Grace has always been a presence in my life, a set of wings to lift me, a shield of light to comfort me. The song is like an angel on my side, serving to bring me to a higher level of consciousness, to center me in thoughts of beauty and hope, to radiate into my own life something of the promise of eternal love. As certainly as the sun coming over the horizon banishes darkness, the song's beauty transforms the listener and lets him, lets her, let go. Trust.

Religion is for those who are afraid of going to hell, I have heard, and the spiritual is for those who have already been there. Poets and ploughmen, mothers and philosophers, sinners and singers alike, each have had their time of confrontation, when they are called to look into their own souls and strike a chord of harmony with divine impulses seemingly far removed from their earthly pursuits. *Amazing Grace* has accompanied many such journeys, and the song's power either to accompany these deep changes or to bring them about is legend. I have also heard, and found to be true in my own life, that what comes from the heart speaks to the heart. "You can't con a con man; you can't deny the truth when it is real." This song must have come from a deep source; authenticity springs from every syllable and touches each heart that hears it—truth to truth, soul to soul. The haunting and yet direct melody of *Amazing Grace* must play some part, as well as the clear, immediately understandable lyric.

When you are weary and without recourse, did you ever notice that just at the moment you can't go on, something happens, some other force takes over, some power greater than yourself, moving you to do the impossible or the unimaginable? *Amazing Grace* reverberates with this truth. Perhaps the "impossible" is getting up in the morning after a night of demon doubts; getting up and going on—the unsung, heroic act of everyone who lives and breathes. Never mind the great triumphs, the moments of brilliant success; it is these mornings, filled with dreamy fog and reluctance to take on the day once again, that produce miracles: people who show up in our lives like angels to guide us, and things that couldn't be said to be reasonably possible that happen to us; sights we see, dreams we dream. *Amazing Grace* is a dream that comes true when I sing it.

I became a singer probably because I needed healing first. My favorite verse of *Amazing Grace* is one I rarely sing in concert, thus keeping its promise personal and universal—somehow the most powerful thing is what you do not tell in the text, holding it like a special talisman of power:

Through many dangers, toils, and snares,
I have already come;
'Tis grace that brought me safe thus far,
And grace will lead me home.

"Grace will lead me home." What a promise. When I recorded *Amazing Grace* in 1970, I felt as though I had known the song forever. My records were selling in the millions, I had many Grammy nominations, and my career was in great shape, but my life was a muddle. I traveled all over the world, and most of the time I felt out of kilter—in the wrong movie, in the wrong script, on the wrong road. From airport to airport and from town to town, I tried not to think about the chaos in my life, holding back the madness like a monster I knew was out there somewhere, outside the windows of the car as it sped on Highway 66 toward Cleveland or Denver or Seattle or Dubuque, often as not fighting with my manager over any little thing, having a hole in the middle of my stomach when I stepped into the hotel room that was so bare and so inhuman, so far far away from everything. And those reviewers and students with their big eyes, how could they know anything or be interested in knowing, even if they said they were?

Demons . . . there were demons everywhere. In the hotel rooms, in the cars, on the planes and the trains. Monsters when I drank, monsters when I didn't drink. Doubts drifted through forests and the plains of the

West, haunting me, following me. I drank then to get beyond them, to get through the day. I understood that life was a battleground, but what did the world know of that inner battle? What if I started screaming in the middle of an interview, "I'm not what you think I am, I'm not who you think I am, I am terrified!" Would they go away with their questions and their intelligent-looking faces, eager, bright, not suffering from the monsters whose faces followed me through Ohio and through Germany?

I was on the edge, getting more and more hysterical as I put on the mask and got up on the stage. I hoisted the guitar around me as though it were a primitive weapon intended to ward off visions of the monsters in the mist of the auditorium. I couldn't see the faces, and always thanked God for that. And the audience, although they could see me, couldn't see what I was thinking between the songs, or they would have left the concert halls in droves; I was sure of that.

The music saved even me, reached even me. I was healed for two hours by the songs I sang and the sense of the presence of other hearts full of their own unsung music, music I was singing for all of us, in spite of myself and my demon. I was reached in spite of myself and then, finally, at the end of the night, I would come to the song that made the monster disappear and gave faces to the crowd; the song that melded us all, each with his or her own monster evaporated for however long the song would last, each of us together in the way we always dreamed of being, me on stage, them out there in the auditorium with their hopes and their ticket stubs and their own dreams. As our voices rose together, we were, each one of us, touched with *Amazing Grace.* With that grace I could get off the stage, find a little relief to get me through the night, and start it all again in the morning.

★ ★ ★ ★

I had always known *Amazing Grace.* I probably first came upon it in the early days of my life in the Methodist church in which I sang for fifteen years, until the "real" music with which I was to make my living was revealed to me. The music at church, like *Amazing Grace,* was not music of the secular world, but music for Sunday morning. By my early twenties I had become very sophisticated and needed Sunday mornings to recover from Saturday nights; there were more and more of both and none of church and the music that went with church.

And yet among the songs about whaling and driving trucks and sporting coal tattoos, my hovering muse always chose spiritual songs as well. In the summer of 1964, during the voter registration drives in the South, I first heard Fanny Lou Hamer's version of *This Little Light of Mine.* I watched her sing while the police waved their billy sticks at her; the rest of us, students and professionals from the North who had hitched rides to Ruleville, Mississippi, to partake in history, would leave the next morning or next week or next month, abandoning the voters to fend for themselves. We would all sing Fanny's song without her.

During those days of turmoil I sang *Amazing Grace* as a rune to give magical protection—a charm to ward off danger, an incantation to the angels of heaven to descend. I had left the choir loft of the Methodists and was not sure magic worked outside of church walls—whether wine would be turned to blood and bread to flesh in the open air in Mississippi. But I wasn't taking any chances.

And grace will lead me home.

How I came to record *Amazing Grace* was a gift I had not foreseen. In the summer of 1969 I was in *Peer Gynt*, playing Solvieg, the long-suffering lover, opposite Stacy Keach. Each night we would entertain sold-out audiences at New York's Delacorte Theater, which resides in the midst of Central Park's leafy trees, pale and full moons, acres of lakes, birds, flowers. The summer in New York, even at its hottest, is sweet in this open-air theater, where the audience sits transformed for a few hours of mystery on the stage, a few blocks from John Lennon's future Strawberry Fields of dreams. Overhead the sky passes but rain seldom forces a cancellation of the show; more often both audience and actors bear the rain, umbrellas up on and off stage.

These nights were unparalleled in my experience. I had never been part of a "group" on stage, and I loved it. After each show, Raul Julia, Sam Waterston, Harris Yulin, James Earl Jones, Olympia Dukakis, who played Anitra in the play, and other friends of Stacy's and mine would go for drinks and dinner, talking and laughing into the night. But before all that, we would always greet our other backstage visitors.

One evening, a tall, handsome, craggy man came backstage with his picture-book wife. He said his name was Roger Payne and introduced his wife as Kate. They'd come back from Bermuda, where they'd made the first underwater recordings of the Great Humpbacked Whales. Kate, like her husband, was beautiful in a way that suggested healthy waters, big skies, and few of the accoutrements of civilization. She was blond with blue eyes and strong-looking hands. She and Roger left me with a quarter-inch reel-to-reel tape of their favorite creatures singing.

"Maybe," Roger said as they departed, "you'll find some use for these singers. I hope so." They were gone and I didn't see much of them for about ten years.

But I got to know the singing whales very well.

By the end of the summer, after *Peer Gynt* was over, I wanted everyone to hear these wonderful singers, as well. So I sang "Farewell to Tarwaithie" over the haunting sound of the whales' voices, and suddenly there was a clear shape to the entire album. Now I knew I would call the album *Whales and Nightingales*. I kept it simple. "Simple Gifts," a traditional song long affiliated with the Shakers, would be on the album. So would a new song of my own, "Nightingale," which I had just written. All the songs but one were chosen, and I racked my brain for something to tie it all together, to make it all complete.

My producer, Mark Abramson, and I had decided in recording this particular album to use acoustically wonderful places to record, instead of working in studios. Taking a remote recording truck, we recorded songs on the stage of Carnegie Hall—can you imagine renting that stage today? We never would have been able to do it!—and the Manhattan Center, and then we were led by our friend, arranger and conductor Joshua Rifkin, to a well-kept secret in New York City, the Chapel of St. Paul's on the Columbia University campus. St. Paul's is a small, elegant, almost mystical little chapel with nearly perfect acoustics. There, under the arcs of green tile, in the light of the stained-glass windows, I asked my friends to join me and sing the only song I knew would be right to complete the album: *Amazing Grace.*

A few weeks after the release of the album in 1970, *Amazing Grace* began to appear on the radio. Everyone knew the song, it seemed, and wanted to hear it. At most gatherings of "folksingers" before this, the evening would end with everyone singing it as a sort of prayer. I had never known any but the first two verses by heart, but there was always someone in the group who knew them all and would line them out for us. But *everyone* always knew the first verse, which we repeated as a chorus, and with a sort of sigh of relief we would all join in: "Amazing grace, how sweet the sound." Now groups of every kind were singing the song together. I was even in an encounter group that ended its sessions with the song. Eerie. Letting go and encountering? Go figure that.

The song was always in my bones, in my genes. I suppose my grandmother Byrd first sang it. She was my mother's mother, a Southerner who had grown up near Nashville in a family whose members often married into clergy. Her sister became a missionary in China; her cousins were ministers in other Protestant sects in the South. Some family members had been Quakers in the previous century, but had drifted through Methodist doors when no silent houses of worship were available, and once Methodist, stayed that way. Some went High Church; later, Episcopal. So certainly my mother, Marjorie, knew *Amazing Grace* long before she met my father in the thirties in Seattle. My dad, Chuck, had his beginnings on a farm in Idaho, somewhere near Nez Perce. There was music in his family: his dad sang, and his uncles played the violin and knew the Irish ballads, and even before my dad went on to become a radio personality and fine singer himself, he knew *Amazing Grace.*

I always thought the song came from the Shaker repertoire, but recently I learned that it was written in the eighteenth century by a man who in his early years gave no indication of having an ounce of grace in his entire body, let alone any "amazing grace" in his soul.

★ ★ ★ ★

John Newton was born in 1725 in England and raised by a tough seafaring father and a devoted and religious mother. In spite of early lessons at his mother's knee, he was a rebellious, contentious teenager and young man who lived the debauched, fragmented life of a libertine, a drunkard and a gambler. His religious upbringing was interrupted by his mother's death when he was seven, and in his spin into blasphemy and the degraded life he developed a scorn for things spiritual as well as a foul tongue. His mother had taught him the Bible stories and how to pray, but he fought the spiritual side of his nature for many years.

In his late teens, Newton became a sailor like his father before him. On board his first ship he fell in with the worst lot, cursing and drinking as they did. He sailed to Venice and back and then, while walking one day near the home of friends he was visiting in Chatham Harbour near London, he was "press-ganged" onto the HMS *Harwich,* bound for the East Indies.

English law at this time had no restraints against the captain of a ship literally grabbing likely looking candidates off the street and putting them to work on board a ship. If you were a tough enough captain, hard-up enough and in need of hands, it was an easy way to staff a vessel. There was no way out for John, who appealed to his father, but by this time his father had had his fill of his son's adolescent personality and thought perhaps hard discipline might do what he had failed to do himself. Newton escaped from the ship on his own, but was discovered and arrested for desertion. Returned to the *Harwich,* he was put in irons, flogged, and demoted. Life among the lowest of the low was worse than ever.

All during even these early stages, Newton appears to have had moments of clarity and repentence. He wrote in his journals of his battles with his demons, and spoke of the remorse that swept over him when, after pledging not to drink, he returned to drinking and violent outbreaks of unfettered anger. Finally, even the captain of the *Harwich* was fed up with Newton's language, his insults, and the disruption he constantly caused on board. He saw a good opportunity to rid himself of Newton, and traded him onto the crew of a slave ship.

Newton was glad to be away from his former captain, and seems to have had no compunction about serving on a ship whose business was moral infamy. The ship's cargo was black men and women, laid foot-to-foot and head-to-head in a pattern in the hold of the ship, which would haunt and torture the soul of even a devoted sinner. Newton apparently gave the "cargo," as he referred to the slaves in his letters from that time, no more thought than bags of wool or stems of bananas. They were his job, not human, and certainly not the equal of any Englishman.

In 1754, on a voyage from London to the shores of Africa, Newton proved himself a good sailor, but as usual he drank heavily and delighted in twisting the words of Scripture learned at his mother's knee. The crew of the *Greyhound,* including even the hardened captain, had never heard such language. They feared John Newton's curses and blasphemy might bring the wrath of God upon the ship and destroy them all.

"Now," Newton was to write later, "the Lord's time was come." One night the crew was awakened by roaring winds, waves pouring over the ship in a violent storm that rocked and threatened to tear the fragile vessel apart. Cries of "She's sinking!" filled the air, shouts and screams of men who were sure they were going to die. John Newton could not swim; as the *Greyhound* split and floundered he somehow made his way to the wheel, lashed himself about the waist and steered the ship through the most awful storm any of his fellow crewmen had ever seen. It was then he began to pray, asking the God his mother had tried to impose upon him as a child to save his soul.

I can imagine John Newton, as you or I would do under the same circumstances, promising God as the wind tore his ship apart and he choked on water from the storm, tied to the wheel with feeble limbs to save himself, that if the Lord would let him live, he would change. On his knees, fearing he was near his last breath, he gave his soul to God. And then in the violence of the storm, not knowing whether he was to live or die, he formed the words of the song that was to become such an anthem of hope in seemingly hopeless situations for so many people in their own storms.

When the winds subsided and the damage was assessed, the crew broke into sobs of relief—they had survived the storm. John Newton had lived through his "bottom," and that transformational spiritual experience, which set out the lines of his life to come, had given birth to *Amazing Grace.*

Still, the work had only begun. He was at a point in which the psyche tips inexorably toward the divine, and in surviving the storm and writing the extraordinary verses to *Amazing Grace,* Newton had found his calling. He determined that he would learn Scripture and become a preacher. He fell back to sin again and again, but as William James's book *The Varieties of Religious Experience* so accurately describes, it was a time of moving sometimes forward, then sliding back, but ever so gradually coming to a total change of the personality. It was agonizing work for John Newton, as it is for everyone. The pull of the spirit won him inch by inch. He studied the Scriptures in Greek and Latin and was eventually offered a ministry to the Olney lacemakers colony near London.

Amazing Grace was included in the *Olney Hymns,* a collection of hundreds of Newton's hymns published late in the century. Many of these new hymns were written in collaboration with Newton's spiritual mentor, William Cowper. *Amazing Grace,* with its lyric by John Newton himself, is the best remembered of any.

The best scholarship on the subject finds the melody of *Amazing Grace* to be from an early Protestant hymn called *New Britain.* As happens in the so-called "folk" tradition, certain verses and slight changes to the lyrics and melody have been made over the past two centuries; different religious sects in many parts of the world have added melodic changes, new words. But the most familiar verses, including the first, which is often repeated as a chorus, are pure, essential Newton.

In his new life as a preacher and writer of hymns, Newton condemned slavery and preached against it for all who listened. His fame spread and people began to come from great distances to hear the "slave trader turned preacher."

"Disagreeable [slavery] I had always found it; but I think I should have quitted it sooner had I considered it as I now do, to be unlawful and wrong," he wrote in diaries near the end of the century. "I hope it will always be a subject of humiliating reflection to me, that I was once an active instrument in a business at which my heart now shudders."

John Newton preached his last sermon in 1806 and died shortly thereafter, leaving behind one of the greatest pieces of music and instruments of salvation ever written. Of the song, we can say, as Newton said of the name of Jesus in one of his last sermons,

It makes the wounded spirit whole
And calms the troubled breast.

Amazing Grace has had a profound effect on many singers. Joan Baez, Jessye Norman, Arlo Guthrie, Aretha Franklin, Sam Cooke; every singer who knows a good melody and a great lyric has sung it at some time. Its sweet directness goes straight to the heart.

In 1989 Bill Moyers produced and hosted a television show called *Amazing Grace,* an in-depth study of the great song. In this moving PBS special, he traced the song's history in light of John Newton's spiritual journey and included the singing of many versions of the song. He and his wife and producer, Judith Moyers, videotaped choruses and individuals, families and church services in which the song is used: Johnny Cash, Jean Ritchie, Jessye Norman, and I all sang versions of *Amazing Grace* and spoke of our feelings about the powerful lyric.

Bill Moyers is a fitting person to have done this piece. An ordained Baptist minister, he has a degree in theology, and his calling in the world has brought him to a ministry that speaks to our deepest longing for content and integrity. His in-depth television coverage of events ranges from the political to the poetic. A spiritual seeker himself, Moyers has made millions of people more aware of the world of their own spirit, and the greatness of *Amazing Grace* led him to want to know more about, and tell us more about, the experience of the song as seen through many performers.

"Where would you like to sing your version of *Amazing Grace*?" Bill asked me as we were preparing to do my part of the special. I told him I thought the best place for my a capella rendition would be in the place I first recorded it, the Chapel of St. Paul's on the campus of Columbia University in New York City.

I arrived at the chapel in a state of déjà vu and, amid the cables and television lights, the cameras, and the pleasure of Bill's amazingly open countenance, I sang the song. It was the first time I had been in the chapel since that recording session twenty years before.

The high green-tiled dome of St. Paul's curves toward heaven. I looked up to the highest point as I sang the song that has carried me through so many "toils and snares." And as I stood in the same light-filled room, singing alone, I remembered that first recording and the friends who had come to sing in the chorus with me—my brother Denver John, and my producer Mark Abramson, and my friend Nancy Bacal, and so many dear companions. This time it was only my own voice, different now from the past nightmare years, my eyes clear and my head not aching—nor my heart—in church on a Thursday afternoon.

Who is to say what happened to that girl who used to sing *Amazing Grace* before the turning point, before a new life that is today's life, free of many of the monsters? Bill Moyers could not have known how this second singing framed the difference. Like Newton, something had happened to me in the midst of the storm. Who is to say what power Newton's beauteous song, which I have sung in concert thousands of times since first recording it, had on that change? Many miracles have happened; who would say why?

I said good-bye to Bill after the shooting and hailed a cab, heading south through Central Park, rolling past John Lennon's Strawberry Fields forever, past the bronze statues of Daniel Webster and Garibaldi. Life goes on—John Lennon knew that, writing and loving, weaving his legend. And of course, John Newton knew it, too. We may not be sure there is life after death, but we are certain there is life after life. We have all seen it for ourselves and we know that something can come to our rescue in the hour of our deepest and darkest need, letting us realize again that miracles are possible, that miracles are the stuff of life, and that what appears real to us is often delusion that can only be addressed by asking God—He or She—to let us in, by letting God do what we cannot. "I can't, She can. I believe I'll let Him."

Amazing Grace transcends religions, cultures, color, geography. People all over the world sing it, as a prayer, as a consolation, as a jewel of great beauty and hope in a world torn with strife. It is the pearl of spiritual songs, produced in the face of sin and desolation and offering hope to each soul who is touched by its profound message.

I once was lost, but now am found
Was blind, but now I see.

—Judy Collins

Amazing grace! (how sweet the sound!)

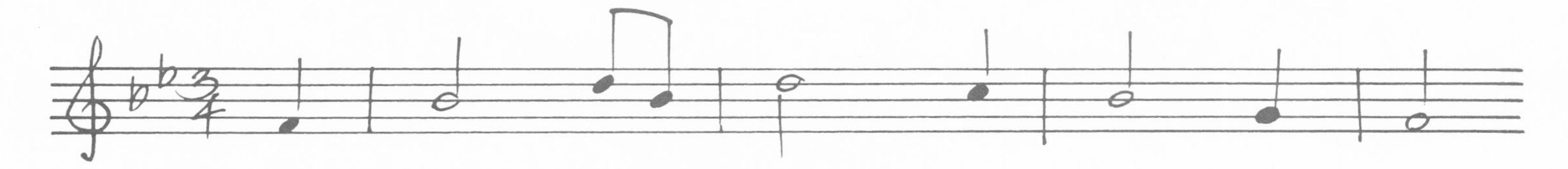

PLEASANT GREEN
BAPtist
CHURCH
A Willis

That sav'd a wretch like me!

I once was lost, but now am found

Was blind, but now I see.

'Twas grace that taught my heart to fear,

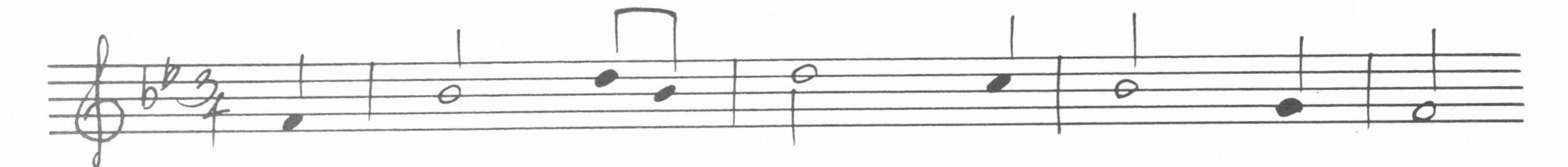

And grace my fears reliev'd;

How precious did that grace appear

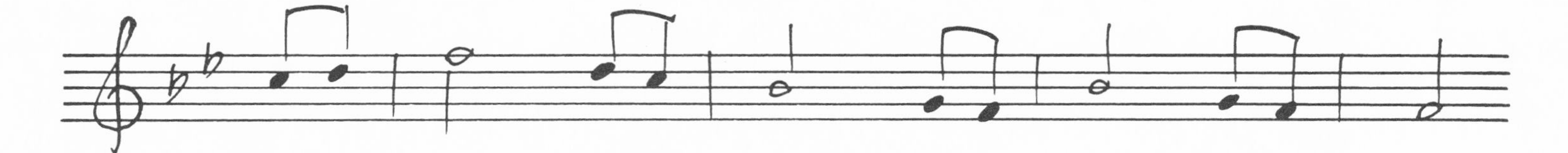

The hour I first believ'd!

Through many dangers, toils, and snares,

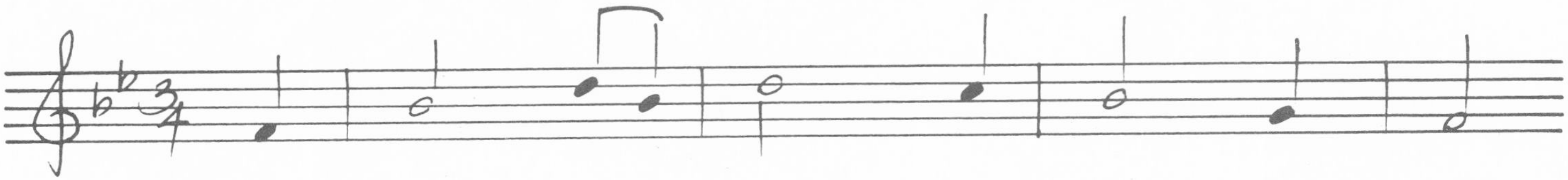

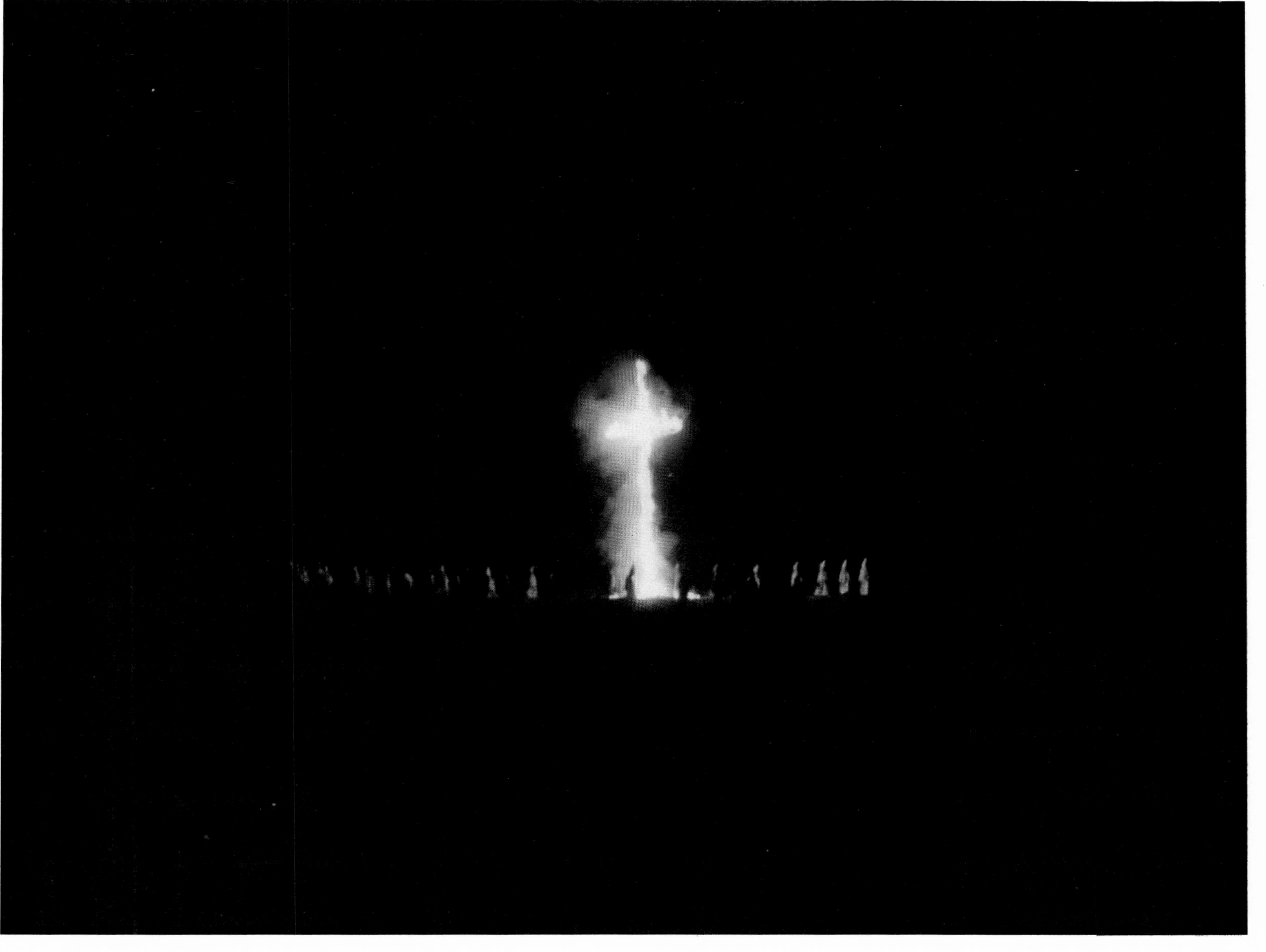

I have already come;

REGISTER TO VOTE
STOP-IN OR CALL HERE
FOR INFORMATION AND FREE RIDE
PHONE 381-7879
IF YOU HAVE MOVED,
OR DID NOT VOTE LAST
THEN YOU MUST
REGISTER
BASIN MINISTRY

'Tis grace that brought me safe thus far,

And grace will lead me home.

The Lord has promis'd good to me,

His word my hope secures;

He will my shield and portion be,

As long as life endures.

Yes, when this flesh and heart shall fail,

LETTERS

And mortal life shall cease;

SACRED
to the memory of
ALICE
wife of
William S. Laboyteaux
who departed this life
March 1st. 1836.
in the 25th. year
of her age.
SACRED
to the memory of
ABIGAIL,
wife of
William S. Laboyteaux
who departed this life
January 5th, 1827,
in the 17th year
of her ag

I shall possess, within the veil,

A life of joy and peace.

The earth shall soon dissolve like snow,

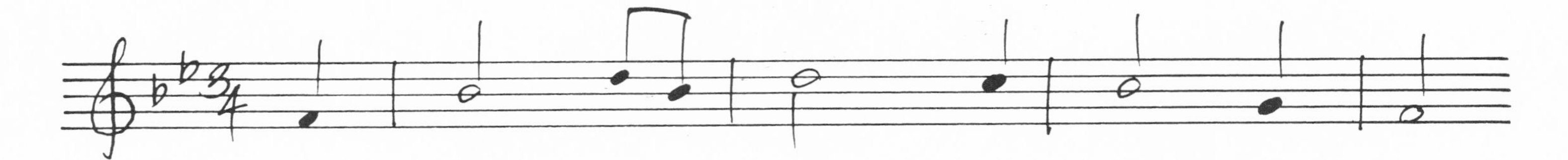

The sun forbear to shine;

But God, who call'd me here below,

Will be forever mine.

AMAZING GRACE

Amazing grace! (how sweet the sound!)
That sav'd a wretch like me!
I once was lost, but now am found
Was blind, but now I see.

'Twas grace that taught my heart to fear,
And grace my fears reliev'd;
How precious did that grace appear
The hour I first believ'd!

Through many dangers, toils, and snares,
I have already come;
'Tis grace that brought me safe thus far,
And grace will lead me home.

The Lord has promis'd good to me,
His word my hope secures;
He will my shield and portion be,
As long as life endures.

Yes, when this flesh and heart shall fail,
And mortal life shall cease;
I shall possess, within the veil,
A life of joy and peace.

The earth shall soon dissolve like snow,
The sun forbear to shine;
But God, who call'd me here below,
Will be forever mine.